Published by:
Candlestick Press,
DiVersity House, 72 Nottingham Road,
Arnold, Nottingham NG5 6LF
www.candlestickpress.co.uk

Design, typesetting, print and production by DiVersity Creative Marketing
Solutions Ltd., www.diversity-nottm.co.uk

Introduction and selection © Carol Ann Duffy, 2012

Cover illustration 'Four Calling Birds' from 'The Twelve Days of Christmas'
© Lizzie Adcock www.arumliliedesigns.co.uk

© Candlestick Press, 2012

ISBN 978 1 907598 14 2

Y821. 92

Acknowledgements:
Our thanks to Nia Dryhurst for her research and our continuing thanks to Carol
Ann Duffy for her generosity and also for her poem 'The Mistletoe Bride'
which is printed here for the first time. Thanks also to Caroline Cook for 'Year
Ending' and Gillian Clarke for 'The Year's Midnight' from *Ice*, Carcanet
Press, 2012. 'Snow' by Louis MacNeice is from *Collected Poems*, Faber &
Faber, 2007, and 'Camels of the Kings' by Leslie Norris is reprinted with the
permission of Dr Meic Stephens © from *The Complete Poems*, Seren, 2008.
'December Stillness'© Siegfried Sassoon is from *Collected Poems*, Faber
& Faber, 1947, and is reprinted by kind permission of the Estate of George
Sassoon. Our thanks to the authors and to Bloodaxe Books for permission
to reprint 'Among Women' by Esther Morgan from *Grace*, Bloodaxe Books,
2011, and 'New Year Behind the Asylum' by David Constantine from *Collected
Poems*, Bloodaxe Books, 2004. 'Various Portents' © Alice Oswald is reprinted
by permission of Faber & Faber from *Woods etc*, Faber & Faber, 2005. 'Planting
Mistletoe' by Ruth Pitter is from *Collected Poems*, Enitharmon Press, 1996,
and is reprinted by permission of Enitharmon Press.

Every effort has been made to trace and contact copyright holders of material
included in this pamphlet. The publisher apologises if any material has been
included without permission or without the appropriate acknowledgement, and
would be glad to be told of anyone who has not been consulted.

Donation to the National Writers' Centre, Tŷ Newydd,
www.literaturewales.org/ty-newydd/

Where poets are no longer living, their dates are given.

Contents   **Page**

Introduction

2012 has been an extraordinary and historic year, and there can be no better way to round it off than with a Christmas of exceptional poetry. It gives me great pleasure to offer this year's selection of twelve poems.

Poetry was never far away from the spotlight during 2012, with a line from Alfred, Lord Tennyson's 'Ulysses' writ large at the London Olympics, the amazing Poetry Parnassus on London's South Bank and sixty newly commissioned poems marking the Queen's Diamond Jubilee.

It has been a year for remembering what came before, and also for delighting in the new and the now. Some of the poems I have chosen are by outstanding contemporary British writers. Others are by old favourites such as Ogden Nash (Santa Claus doubters watch out) and, again, Alfred, Lord Tennyson. After the national bell-ringing back in the summer, it seemed a good moment to include 'Ring out, wild bells' with its sometimes forgotten message of decency and hope, public and private:

> Ring out false pride in place and blood,
> The civic slander and the spite;
> Ring in the love of truth and right,
> Ring in the common love of good.

This year, Candlestick Press will be making a donation to the National Writers' Centre, Tŷ Newydd, which offers a wide variety of residential creative writing courses and experiences to people of all ages and backgrounds.

Finally, it remains only to welcome you to 'the gold tree', 'the silver seed' and other 'beautiful works in bronze' that follow in these pages and to wish you

Merry Christmas!

Carol Ann Duffy

Among Women*

One evening I came back home
and everything was just as I'd left it –

except the bowls gleamed with a new knowledge,
the cat wore his yellow gaze like a mask,

and I sensed the house had been visited –
wings unfurling like ferns in the quiet air.

I was blessed with children anyway,
I shook my life out like a cloth,

and perhaps there is a purpose after all
in not being chosen:

the minute my clock has never regained,
sunlight in the guest room climbing its ladder of dust.

Esther Morgan

*title from the story of the Annunciation as told in St Luke's Gospel, Ch.1, v.28:
'And the angel came in unto her, and said, Hail, thou that art highly favoured,
the Lord is with thee: blessed art thou among women.'

Various Portents

Various stars. Various kings.
Various sunsets, signs, cursory insights.
Many minute attentions, many knowledgeable watchers,
Much cold, much overbearing darkness.

Various long midwinter Glooms.
Various Solitary and Terrible Stars.
Many Frosty Nights, many previously Unseen
    Sky-flowers.
Many people setting out (some of them kings) all clutching at
    stars.

More than one North Star, more than one South Star.
Several billion elliptical galaxies, bubble nebulae, binary
    systems,
Various dust lanes, various routes through varying thicknesses of
    Dark,
Many tunnels into deep space, minds going back and forth.

Many visions, many digitally enhanced heavens,
All kinds of glistenings being gathered into telescopes:
Fireworks, gasworks, white-streaked works of Dusk,
Works of wonder and/or water, snowflakes, stars of frost ...

Various dazed astronomers dilating their eyes,
Various astronauts setting out into laughterless earthlessness,
Various 5,000-year-old moon maps,
Various blindmen feeling across the heavens in braille.

Various gods making beautiful works in bronze,
Brooches, crowns, triangles, cups and chains,
And all sorts of drystone stars put together without mortar.
Many Wisemen remarking the irregular weather.

Many exile energies, many low-voiced followers,
Watchers of wisps of various glowing spindles,
Soothsayers, hunters in the High Country of the Zodiac,
Seafarers tossing, tied to a star...

Various people coming home (some of them kings). Various
    headlights.
Two or three children standing or sitting on the low wall.
Various winds, the Sea Wind, the sound-laden Winds of
    Evening
Blowing the stars towards them, bringing snow.

Alice Oswald

Camels of the Kings

The Camels, the Kings' Camels, Haie-aie!
Saddles of polished leather, stained red and purple,
Pommels inlaid with ivory and beaten gold,
Bridles of silk embroidery, worked with flowers.
The Camels, the Kings' Camels!

We are groomed with silver combs,
We are washed with perfumes.
The grain of richest Africa is fed to us,
Our dishes are silver.
Like cloth-of-gold glisten our sleek pelts.
Of all camels, we alone carry the Kings!
Do you wonder that we are proud?
That our hooded eyes are contemptuous?

As we sail past the tented villages
They beat their copper gongs after us.
The windswifts, the desert racers, see them!
Faster than gazelles, faster than hounds,
Haie-aie! The Camels, the Kings' Camels!
The sand drifts in puffs behind us,
The glinting quartz, the fine, hard grit.
Do you wonder that we look down our noses?
Do you wonder we flare our superior nostrils?

All night we have run under the moon,
Without effort, breathing lightly,
Smooth as a breeze over the desert floor,
One white star our compass.
We have come to no palace, no place
Of towers and minarets and the calling of servants,
But a poor stable in a poor town.
So why are we bending our crested necks?
Why are our heads bowed
And our eyes closed meekly?
Why are we outside this hovel,
Humbly and awkwardly kneeling?
How is it that we know the world is changed?

Leslie Norris (1921 – 2006)

Snow

The room was suddenly rich and the great bay-window was
Spawning snow and pink roses against it
Soundlessly collateral and incompatible:
World is suddener than we fancy it.

World is crazier and more of it than we think,
Incorrigibly plural. I peel and portion
A tangerine and spit the pips and feel
The drunkenness of things being various.

And the fire flames with a bubbling sound for world
Is more spiteful and gay than one supposes –
On the tongue on the eyes on the ears in the palms of one's
        hands –
There is more than glass between the snow and the huge roses.

Louis MacNeice (1907 – 1963)

The Boy who laughed at Santa Claus

In Baltimore there lived a boy.
He wasn't anybody's joy.
Although his name was Jabez Dawes,
His character was full of flaws.
In school he never led his classes,
He hid old ladies' reading glasses,
His mouth was open when he chewed,
And elbows to the table glued.

He stole the milk of hungry kittens,
And walked through doors marked NO ADMITTANCE.
He said he acted thus because
There wasn't any Santa Claus.
Another trick that tickled Jabez
Was crying 'Boo!' at little babies.
He brushed his teeth, they said in town,
Sideways instead of up and down.

Yet people pardoned every sin,
And viewed his antics with a grin,
Till they were told by Jabez Dawes,
'There isn't any Santa Claus!'
Deploring how he did behave,
His parents swiftly sought their grave.
They hurried through the portals pearly,
And Jabez left the funeral early.

Like whooping cough, from child to child,
He sped to spread the rumor wild:
'Sure as my name is Jabez Dawes
There isn't any Santa Claus!'
Slunk like a weasel or a marten
Through nursery and kindergarten,
Whispering low to every tot:
'There isn't any, no there's not!'

The children wept all Christmas Eve
And Jabez chortled up his sleeve.
No infant dared hang up his stocking
For fear of Jabez' ribald mocking.
He sprawled on his untidy bed,
Fresh malice dancing in his head,
When presently with scalp a-tingling,
Jabez heard a distant jingling;
He heard the crunch of sleigh and hoof
Crisply alighting on the roof.

What good to rise and bar the door?
A shower of soot was on the floor.
What was beheld by Jabez Dawes?
The fire-place full of Santa Claus!
Then Jabez fell upon his knees
With cries of 'Don't,' and 'Pretty please.'
He howled: 'I don't know where you read it,
But anyhow, I never said it!'

'Jabez,' replied the angry saint,
'It isn't I, it's you that ain't.
Although there is a Santa Claus,
There isn't any Jabez Dawes!'
Said Jabez then with impudent vim,
'Oh, yes there is! and I am him!
Your magic don't scare me, it doesn't'—
And suddenly he found he wasn't!

From grimy feet to grimy locks,
Jabez became a Jack-in-the-box,
An ugly toy with springs unsprung,
For ever sticking out his tongue.
The neighbours heard his mournful squeal;
They searched for him but not with zeal.
No trace was found of Jabez Dawes,
Which led to thunderous applause,
And people drank a loving cup
And went and hung their stockings up.

All you who sneer at Santa Claus,
Beware the fate of Jabez Dawes,
The saucy boy who mocked the saint.
Donder and Blitzen licked off his paint.

Ogden Nash (1902 – 1971)

December Stillness

December stillness, teach me through your trees
That loom along the west, one with the land,
The veiled evangel of your mysteries.
While nightfall, sad and spacious, on the down
Deepens, and dusk imbues me, where I stand,
With grave diminishings of green and brown,
Speak, roofless Nature, your instinctive words;
And let me learn your secret from the sky,
Following a flock of steadfast-journeying birds
In lone remote migration beating by.
December stillness, crossed by twilight roads,
Teach me to travel far and bear my loads.

Siegfried Sassoon (1886 – 1967)

Year Ending

Cold has spelled the garden while we were sleeping
and has turned the soil to embers, witched the leaves
to rust. Overnight clouds of white blossom

like ruffs have come to the arms of trees. The lawn
is ashen, pinned-out, scared to stiffness
and a hoarfrost tells the spiders' secrets, lacing stalk

to stalk like rigging thickly roped, catching
the rays of early sun. The willow weeps
with frozen diamond tears; so the garden

has not been banished but is coming back obliquely,
tranced at rakish angles – still alive but altered,
and a charged light, snowlight, picks out other themes

– the wafer-pennied honesty along scant lines,
dark, brittle seedcrowns with their architecture
underplayed before, and orange blobs of physalis

that smoulder grounded. Clutches of berries hang on tightly
to the firethorn. Dogwood reddens. The cotoneaster stretches out
its fishbone limbs. An intimate is stranger – grown contrary.

Still, there is wit in icicles zigzagging gutters like a dragon's grin
and candyfloss caught on the beech, pompoms of mistletoe,
and snow like icing freshly piped along bare branches.

Caroline Cook

Planting Mistletoe

Let the old tree be the gold tree;
Hand up the silver seed:
Let the hoary tree be the glory tree,
To shine out at need,
At mirth-time, at dearth-time,
Gold bough and milky bead.

For the root's failing and the shoot's failing;
Soon it will bloom no more.
The growth's arrested, the yaffle's nested
Deep in its hollow core:
Over the grasses thinly passes
The shade so dark before.

Save a few sprigs of the new twigs,
If any such you find:
Don't lose them, but use them,
Keeping a good kind
To be rooting and fruiting
When this is old and blind.

So the tragic tree is the magic tree,
Running the whole range
Of growing and blowing
And suffering change:
Then buying, by dying,
The wonderful and strange.

Ruth Pitter (1897 – 1992)

The Year's Midnight

The flown, the fallen,
the golden ones,
the deciduous dead, all gone
to ground, to dust, to sand,
borne on the shoulders of the wind.

Listen! They are whispering
now while the world talks,
and the ice melts,
and the seas rise.
Look at the trees!

Every leaf-scar is a bud
expecting a future.
The earth speaks in parables.
The burning bush. The rainbow.
Promises. Promises.

Gillian Clarke

New Year Behind the Asylum

There was the noise like when the men in droves
Are hurrying to the match only this noise was
Everybody hurrying to see the New Year in
In town under the clock but we, that once,

He said would I come our usual Saturday walk
And see it in out there in the open fields
Behind the asylum. Even on sunny days
How it troubled me more and more the nearer we got

And he went quiet and as if he was ashamed
For what he must always do, which was
Go and grip the bars of the iron gates and stand
Staring into the garden until they saw him.

They were like the animals, so glad and shy
Like overgrown children dressed in things
Handed down too big or small and they came in a crowd
And said hello with funny chunnering noises

And through the bars, looking so serious,
He put his empty hand out. But that night
We crept past quickly and only stopped
In the middle of the empty fields and there

While the clock in the square where the normal people stood
And all the clocks in England were striking twelve
We heard the rejoicings for the New Year
From works and churches and the big ships in the docks

So faint I wished we were hearing nothing at all
We were so far away in our black fields
I felt we might not ever get back again
Where the people were and it was warm, and then

Came up their sort of rejoicing out of the asylum,
Singing or sobbing I don't know what it was
Like nothing on earth, their sort of welcoming in
Another New Year and it was only then

When the bells and the cheerful hooters couldn't be heard
But only the inmates, only the poor mad people
Singing or sobbing their hearts out for the New Year
That he gripped me fast and kissed my hair

And held me in against him and clung on tight to me
Under a terrible number of bare stars
So far from town and the lights and house and home
And shut my ears against the big children crying

But listened himself, listened and listened
That one time. And I've thought since and now
He's dead I'm sure that what he meant was this:
That I should know how much love would be needed.

David Constantine

'Ring out, wild bells'

Ring out, wild bells, to the wild sky,
    The flying cloud, the frosty light:
    The year is dying in the night;
Ring out, wild bells, and let him die.

Ring out the old, ring in the new,
    Ring, happy bells, across the snow:
    The year is going, let him go;
Ring out the false, ring in the true.

Ring out the grief that saps the mind,
    For those that here we see no more;
    Ring out the feud of rich and poor,
Ring in redress to all mankind.

Ring out a slowly dying cause,
    And ancient forms of party strife;
    Ring in the nobler modes of life,
With sweeter manners, purer laws.

Ring out the want, the care, the sin,
    The faithless coldness of the times;
    Ring out, ring out my mournful rhymes,
But ring the fuller minstrel in.

Ring out false pride in place and blood,
    The civic slander and the spite;
    Ring in the love of truth and right,
Ring in the common love of good.

Ring out old shapes of foul disease;
    Ring out the narrowing lust of gold;
    Ring out the thousand wars of old,
Ring in the thousand years of peace.

Ring in the valiant man and free,
    The larger heart, the kindlier hand;
    Ring out the darkness of the land,
Ring in the Christ that is to be.

Alfred, Lord Tennyson (1809 – 1892)

The Mistletoe Bride

The December bride who, bored
with dancing, skipped from the castle hall
to play hide-and-seek, a white bird
flickering into the dark...

                                 The groom,
who searched each room, calling
her name; then the bridal guests,
flame-lit, checking the grounds...

The fifty Christmases till a carpenter
jemmied an old oak chest; the skeleton
with its unstrung pearls, loose emeralds,
its rings of diamond, sapphire, gold...

The running feet, the shouting for others
to see what he'd seen; mistletoe
in the loose bones of a hand...
like love, patiently green.

Carol Ann Duffy